MEASHAM IN FOCUS

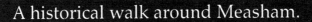

A historical walk around Measham.

Edited by
K. Elliott & J. L. Salter

Measham Village History Group

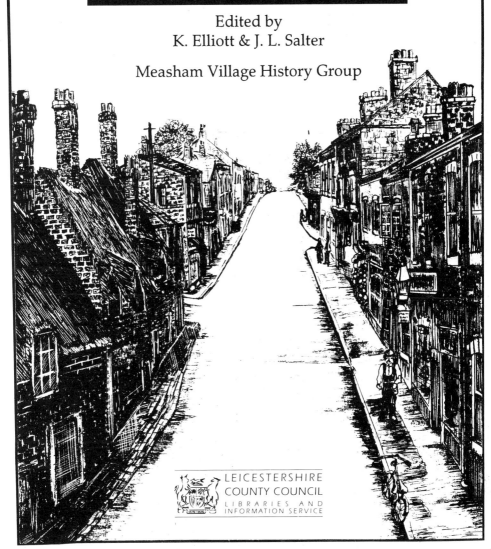

LEICESTERSHIRE
COUNTY COUNCIL
LIBRARIES AND
INFORMATION SERVICE

PREFACE

The publication is, we hope, the first, but not the last, produced by the Measham Village History Research Group. The group had its origins in an initiative from Measham Parish Council in 1988, which was followed by a talk from Dr. Marylyn Palmer of the University of Leicester, and an approach from the Parish Council to the University Adult Education Department. The rest was an adult class, jointly sponsored by the Department and the Ivanhoe Community College, which has met in the Autumn and Spring Terms since then, and for which Dr. Salter has been the tutor.

It must be emphasised that this is very much a group product, and it will be appreciated that only with much research and investigation by group members and others is a publication of this sort possible, especially in a place where much of the visual evidence has disappeared, a fact which many would regret. Special thanks must, however, be paid to Mr. Frank Sharrod who has been a loyal member of the group, and who has made his unrivalled knowledge of the history of Measham and its people available to us. We have had also the advantage of being able to draw on his impressive collection of Measham photographs and memorabilia. Mrs. Mary Hill has made available her considerable local knowledge as well as the large collection of press-cuttings from the first decades of this century which are in her possession.

Mr. N. Haddock has done considerable work on the 'Wilkes period' of the history of Measham, some of which it is hoped will be published elsewhere, and has contributed the introduction to this publication. Mr. K. Elliott made himself responsible for the onerous task of collating the photographic archive which the group built up and helping the group in selection of material. The text is based on his initial draft. It must again be stressed, however, that the accuracy of the text (and the range of photographs) would have suffered without the group as a whole and their hard work.

In addition to the above, the other members of the group who have been concerned with the photographic history are: Mrs M Jerrams, Mrs M Marcini, Mrs M Onion, Mrs P Page, Miss M Price, Mr and Mrs JG Shilliam, Mr E Turner and Mr H Wright.

The group would like to thank the following for permission to reproduce photographs in their possession.

Mr W Ball	Mr E Hayes	Mrs J Nelson
Mrs L Bradford	Miss L Hayle	Mr G Nutt
Mr R Carter	Mrs N Higham	Mr G Ridgeway
Mrs B Clamp	Mrs M Hill	Mr F Sharrod
Mr K Elliott	Mrs M Jerrams	Mr J Shilliam
Mr T Goode	Mr R O Jones	Mrs J Sorer
Mr T Hart	Mrs M Marcini	Mrs M Statham
The late Dr J Hart	Mrs M Maynard	Dr M Tellis

The Red Bank Manufacturing Company

The Deacons and Trustees, Measham Baptist Church

Mrs Marion Alexander of Mancetter, Warwickshire, gave invaluable help in re-photographing prints to a professional standard but at a less than professional cost!

Many thanks are due to Mrs Kate Waring who specially drew the sketch used on the title page.

For permission to reproduce the painting by Villiac (page 113 and back cover) the group would like to thank Mrs Susan Matthews, daughter of the late Dr. J. Hart. For help with photographing the paintings, thanks are due to Mrs Heather Tellis and Mr Robert Owen Jones.

The group would be very pleased to hear from anyone who can supply more information on any of the photographs included here, or indeed, can correct any information given. Similarly, we are always pleased to hear of other photographs which could be included in a future work.

Finally, the group would like to thank all who have contributed in any way to this publication and would like to make special mention of Measham Parish Council whose generous financial help has enabled the work to be produced much more readily and more cheaply than would otherwise have been the case. The ready cooperation of Leicestershire County Library in the production of this work has been very much appreciated.

INTRODUCTION

The name of the village suggests that it was an Anglo-Saxon settlement deriving its name from its location near the river Mease. Viking settlements were common in this area, as other place-names show.

With the coming of the Normans and with a very brief entry in the Domesday Book, the village became a feudal unit where agricultural and other rights were owned by a series of absentee Lords of the Manor.

Repton Priory held lands within the Manor, and its monks rebuilt the parish church in nearly its present form about the year 1300. Records show that this rather large church then served a large and thriving community which supported a weekly market, and was occasionally visited by the Court of Assize.

Plainly Measham was an agrarian centre in a surrounding district of bleak heathland covered with gorse and bracken. But the heathland offered wealth to the Lords of Measham Manor and their lessees, in the form of the shallow and outcropping seams of coal which were among the earliest mining sites in Britain, from the 1200s and possibly before. These sites to the North and West of Measham were exploited fairly continuously until the surface seams were worked out and mining moved towards Donisthorpe and the Wolds in the late 1700s.

For reasons which it is still hard to understand the town of Measham had a big drop in population between 1400 - 1600. When the Wollastons bought the Manor of Measham in 1643 with its 1,000 acres, it had 12 tenanted cottages and houses, and population of perhaps 50 people. However, there is evidence that there may have been 300 to 400 miners working locally at that time and attending the parish church, and that these lived in temporary shanty settlements near the mines. The Wollaston family succeeded the Bedfords, the Lords Sheffield and the Anderson family, who had all held the manor previously. They owned nearly all the land in the village, and enclosed the common fields between Measham Hall and Measham House in 1750. They sold the manor to Joseph Wilkes in 1777.

When Wilkes and his brothers acquired the Manor, about 400 acres (extending to Oakthorpe and Hartshorne) had been added, and the population had a total of about 220 tenants and their families. Leather was the only non-mining industry and was centred on the Tanyard area of High Street.

Wilkes transformed the fortunes and size of Measham. Encouraged by his business enterprises the population grew from 220 to 1,600 in the years 1777-1809.

The Industrial Revolution in Measham is of some historical importance and is inseparable from the name of Joseph Wilkes (1732-1805) of Overseal. Wilkes came from a family of agricultural factors who had interests in turnpike road building, canal construction (the Burton Boat Co.) and local banking. He himself was associated with the Peel family in their cotton enterprises at Burton and Tamworth, and in their London bank. In 1777, Wilkes and his two brothers bought the Manor at Measham from Sir William Wollaston for £56,000.

In the utilitarian spirit of the age he was determined to develop the tiny mining village of clay hovels into a model industrial and agricultural community. He made advances in manufacture, mineral extraction and farming, achieving these with the aid of machinery and improved communications.

In mineral extraction he sank several new coal mines in the area, and worked them to unprecedented depths. In 1787 he was the first man to employ steam winding with a Boulton and Watt engine, at his Nether Leys colliery. In the same year he had installed a similar engine for the grinding of corn at a mill on the High Street of Measham (only the second such use). Wilkes also processed lime from Calke and Cloud Hill at his kilns at Ilotts Wharf, supplying much of Leicestershire and the Midlands. In manufacture, he brought cotton to Measham, where he used an existing watermill on Atherstone Road for bleaching, built a new spinning mill in 1782 (aided by steam) on the Tamworth Road, and in 1802 constructed a carding mill with a huge 30 horse-power Boulton and Watt engine adjacent to the corn mill on High Street. These last two mills were destroyed by fire in 1901 and 1836 respectively.

In agriculture Wilkes experimented with farm machinery, the use of manures and fertilizers, land irrigation, underground housing of livestock and breed improvement in cattle and sheep. He became the first president of the Smithfield Society.

In communications Wilkes improved the potential for marketing his products by building more turnpike roads on the 'concave' surface principle for better drainage. This system was later adopted by the railways for their tracks.

Wilkes also instituted in Measham a system of horse-drawn tramways to transport lime or coal to the turnpikes or to the Ashby-de-la-Zouch canal, which company he represented as Secretary and Treasurer during its construction (1794-1804). The canal was intended primarily to convey coal from the developing mines of the Ashby Wolds, through an 18 mile course without locks to the Coventry canal, and thence to the markets of the South East.

All the developments by Wilkes supported a system of mortgaging real property and of local banks to take in funds. These included the banks of Measham and Ashby.

Unfortunately, by 1820-1835 Wilkes' various enterprises had largely stagnated or ceased operation and the Manor was sold to Lord Hastings. Wilkes' family and successors lacked his entrepreneurial flair, but other geographical and economic factors came into play, not the least being the failure and bankruptcy of the banking interest.

However, there are still many visual reminders in the village of the Wilkes presence in the giant double size bricks which were used in the construction and re-construction of houses, shops and workplaces. The bricks were made locally to mitigate the effect of the brick tax (1785-1804).

Wilkes old colliery of Measham Fields which re-opened in the 1850s boosted production greatly about 1890, and this inaugurated a period of new prosperity and employment growth for the village. In the early 1900s there followed the opening of the shoe factory and the beginning of the clay-related industries at Coronet and Red Bank. The late 1940s saw the opening the of the car auctions and more recently the Westminster Industrial Estate which contains a number of different enterprises. There are current plans to augment these and to secure the economic well-being of Measham for the foreseeable future.

NOTE ON ARRANGEMENT OF PHOTOGRAPHS

After some discussion, the group decided to arrange the photographs not in topics, but as a 'walk round the village', starting at the parish church. To assist those not familiar with Measham, the following list will be helpful, as will the map of the village which follows.

Parish Church, and vicarage northwards;
Adjacent parts of High Street,
Saracen's Lane
Queen Street   pages   9 - 29

Leicester Road (Swepstone Road)
Colliery
Measham Hall and Clock Mill   pages 30 - 50

High Street (North)
New Road End
Ashby Road to Five Lane Ends   pages 51 - 61

High Street (Church-Bosworth Road)
Bosworth Road
St Charles' Church
Chapel Street
High Street   pages 62 - 90

Ashby Canal
Lower High Street
Railway
Athershone road
'Red Bank'
Measham Car Auctions
Tamworth Road (The Avenue)   pages 91 - 143

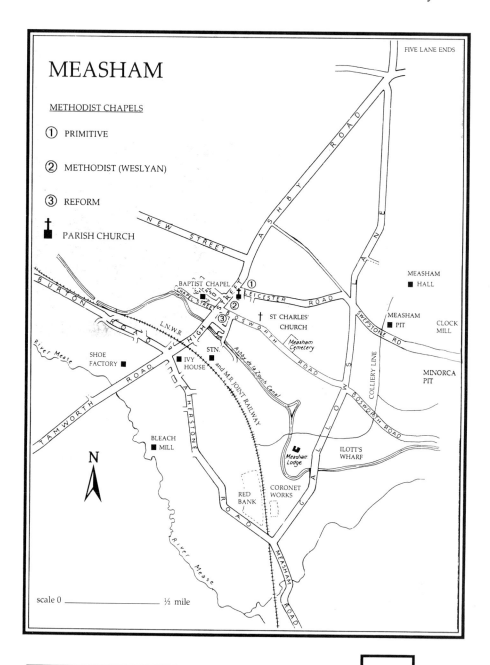

MEASHAM

METHODIST CHAPELS

① PRIMITIVE

② METHODIST (WESLYAN)

③ REFORM

✝ PARISH CHURCH

FIVE LANE ENDS

ASHBY ROAD

LANE

NEW STREET

MEASHAM HALL

BAPTIST CHAPEL

LEICESTER ROAD

BURTON ROAD

L.N.W.R

CHAPEL STREET

HIGH STREET

① ② ③

BOSWORTH ROAD

✝ ST CHARLES' CHURCH

Measham Cemetery

SWEPSTONE RD.

MEASHAM PIT

CLOCK MILL

River Mease

SHOE FACTORY

STN.

IVY HOUSE

Abbey de la Zouch Canal

COLLIERY LINE

W. BOSWORTH ROAD

MINORCA PIT

TAMWORTH ROAD

and M.R JOINT RAILWAY

ATHERSTONE ROAD

BLEACH MILL

Measham Lodge

ILOTT'S WHARF

N

RED BANK

CORONET WORKS

GALLOWS

River Mease

MEASHAM ROAD.

scale 0 ⸻ ½ mile

Measham Parish Church about 1904.

The church was for many years the hub of village life, and it still gives many people a feeling of something reassuring and familiar. It was rebuilt, circa 1340, by the monks of Repton Priory; a large church for a village of Measham's size at that time.

Parish Church, Measham.

The church from the west about 1910.

The blocked-up west door and the corner of the then vicarage may be clearly seen.

Vicarage, built by Joseph Wilkes about 1790.

This was a large three-storied building running parallel to the church drive. The front door faced High Street, and was entered up a few steps from the pavement. Built of Wilkes' famous 'jumb' bricks, it had the distinctive curved-top recessed windows. The photograph shows the vicarage from the church drive. It was demolished about 1960 after standing empty for some time after the new vicarage was built in 1955.

The Reverend J. Hewitson.

In his time, the household employed local girls as domestic servants. Joseph Hewitson succeeded his father, who originally came from Hull, in 1893. He was born in Measham in 1860 and was vicar until 1924. He had a brother James and two sisters, one of whom (Ruth) was president of the local branch of the Women's Temperance Society.

A double wedding in 1897.

The bridegroom on the left is the Reverend Mr. Appleton from The Laurels at the top of High Street; his bride is Miss Hewitson, the daughter of the late vicar. The bridegroom on the right is Mr. James Hewitson, his son, and the bride is Miss Mary Bonas.

High Street seen from the Queen's Head 1907.

The vicarage is the tall building in the centre of the photograph showing its front door and the steps leading up from the pavement. The large tree is in the vicarage garden with its high wall running down to the church drive. The photograph distinctly shows again the Wilkes' trademark of using recessed arches particularly above windows and doors.

The three boys standing on the edge of the pavement in front of the Queen's Head are wearing their 'long' short trousers and caps. The lady walking up the street in front of Cross House with her apron flowing in the breeze reminds one of the fashions of earlier days. Notice the gas lamp fixed to the corner of the Queen's Head, and the large sign over the front door advertising Burton Ales and Stout.

The 1906 Infirmary Parade.

The parade took place on a Sunday when local and guest organisations paraded through the streets to collect money for the hospitals used by Measham people, at Leicester, Ashby and Burton.

The Parade in the High Street.

The Infirmary Parade started in 1901 and continued up to the Second World War. After the war contributions came from the churches in the form of collections from events such as Harvest Festivals. The parade and church service collection which took place in 1919 realised £90.2s.0d. After expenses it was decided to send £71.17s.6d. to Leicester Royal Infirmary and £10 to the Ashby Cottage Hospital.

After the Parade.

Here can be clearly seen the chemist's shop, then under the ownership of Mr. Holt. The house on the extreme left is at the end of Saracens' Row.

The Measham butcher, with his horse.

Above the chemist's shop is Saracen's Lane. This lane passed the slaughter house and cottages of Mr. Ball the butcher, seen here with one of his horses. The Ball family has long been, and still is, associated with the butchery trade.

opposite page
Iveagh House, formerly Croft House.

At the end of the lane was a fine house and outbuildings, known as Iveagh House. This was well known as the residence and surgery of Doctor Hart. As may be seen, it was a substantial house with its flowering climber at the front and fruit tree at the side. The house was originally a farm called Croft House, probably an enlarged much older property.

Croft House was purchased by Doctor G.S. Hart in 1899 for the sum of £1000. The property included the outbuildings and three acres of land. The name Iveagh House was given to the property by Doctor Hart senior after a town in Northern Ireland, as he had come over to England from there. The barn was converted into a surgery in 1906 and it remained so until 1967 when the property was demolished to build Iveagh Close. Iveagh Close was built by Fred Hart and Son, an old established family of builders in Measham.

Dr. Hart, senior, with Rocket.

The practice at Iveagh House was carried on by Dr. Hart and his son Jack for many years. They were both much respected and liked by the community.

The Measham and district ambulance.

The vehicle was bought by contributions from the people of Measham as a memorial to Dr. G.S. Hart in 1923. The ambulance was a Dodge, originally with solid tyres, changed later to pneumatic tyres to give the patient a more comfortable ride. The cost of the ambulance was £418.16s.0d. The colliery company acquired the ambulance in about 1940 and used it until 1942. Its last journey with a patient ended in disaster while taking a miner with an injured leg to Leicester Infirmary. On this journey it broke down and the patient continued his journey on a fruiterer's lorry.

Sarah Whetton, midwife, at her doorstep 107 High Street.

Mrs. Whetton helped Doctor Hart senior with looking after his patients and also acted as the local midwife. She was said to have delivered over 2000 babies.

opposite page
The fire brigade posing for the camera in the yard of Iveagh House.

The fire station was on the right at the lower end of Queen Street, which is opposite the church, and was until recently known as Cross Street. It was a busy place, as for many years weekly markets were held there. Round the square itself were the Queen's public house, the Red Lion, the school, two butchers' shops (Mr. Ball's and Mr. Hinks') as well as a number of cottages and the fire station.

The fire station had high curved-topped doors, and the roof was surmounted by a belfry which housed the fire bell. The fire bell had an earlier life at the mill complex of Joseph Wilkes on Tamworth Road, dating back to 1783. The bell chimed the hour of the mill clock and possibly could be tolled by hand to call the shifts to work. The bell now has another resting place, on the left along the church drive.

The fire brigade was started before 1894; a secondhand engine was purchased in 1905 and the old one sold. The number of firemen was 12 except during the First World War when only 8 were recruited. Members of the team were appointed by the Parish Council, and were paid on a call-out basis, with the rate depending on the distance travelled to the fire. The fire brigade must have been quite a sight galloping along the street - that is, after the horses had been caught. It would appear that there was a pump and an escape ladder to be pulled by the horses. In this photograph, the fire hoses and branch are neatly stacked beside the pump and the men are standing smartly to attention, helmets no doubt well polished.

The teachers shown are: left to right standing. Mrs. Edna Pickering, Fred Harrison (student teacher), Mr. Evans and Mr. Hambleton. Sitting, Miss Peach, Mr. Charles Higham (Headmaster) and Miss Jones.

Teachers at Queen Street, outside the Headmaster's house in 1938 or 1939.

The school in Queen Street will have varying memories for many ex-pupils. Built in 1829 and extended in 1833, the school was visited in 1839 by Queen Adelaide, the street having its name changed to commemorate this occasion. A plaque is situated inside the building and the inscription reads: "In Memoria Habere, on the 25 day of October 1839, Adelaide the Queen Dowager and suite visited this institution. When Her Majesty, intimating an anxious interest for the welfare of the schools was graciously pleased to express her high approbation of their state and efficiency and the manner in which they have been conducted. 'Fear God: Honour the King: Persevere'". The building closed as a school in 1977 and opened as a community centre in 1982.

Tending the allotments.

When boys stayed at Measham school until school-leaving age, woodwork and gardening formed an important part of their activities. These allotments ran down alongside the gully.

Entertainment for demobilised forces in 1919.

The school was used for various functions and festivities. On this occasion the demobilised soldiers and sailors were entertained by their fellow residents on 9 August 1919. The company included men who had served in South Africa, India and the Sudan.

Meeting in the Market Place (Queen Street) at 1.30 p.m. the ex-servicemen and committee members paraded the flag-bedecked streets headed by Ibstock Town band. After dinner the large company stood in silence honouring the memory of those who had lost their lives. Later they joined in musical entertainment provided by local artists accompanied by Mr. A. Lewin.

Another view of this patriotic and poignant occasion.

In the evening medals for bravery were presented by Lt. Col. German, D.S.O. Military medals were presented to former Privates William Pickering (5th Leicesters) and J.T. Wilman (5th Gloucesters). The Military Medal awarded posthumously to Sgt R. Ensor, killed action in France, was received by his father, Mr William Ensor.

From the Queen's Head at the corner of Queen Street, looking up High Street.

This photograph (another from the Infirmary Parade of 1906) shows right to left, Mr Arthur Jewsbury's fish shop, the general store of Mr Badcock, the dwelling of Mr Emerson and the shop of Mr Ernest Easom the shoe repairer, later used at the Liberal Club but now demolished.

Swepstone Road junction was much narrower in the past, as perhaps can be seen from the space between Mr Easom's shop and the tall three storey block of houses on the other side of the road. In this block lived Mr Ezra Atkins (lamplighter), Police Sergeant Wood and Mr Jack Ball. The white building next to this block is the Swan public house with a man standing on top of the large bay window.

The Church Parade of 1911.

The parade is in Queen Street, outside the Queen's Head and Joshua Hinks' shop. Notice people looking out of the upstairs windows of the Queen's Head and Cross House. The band boys are wearing pill box hats. It was probably the Desford Boys' Band which played on the occasion.

Malt House Well.

Opposite Swepstone Road (Leicester Road) junction was the imposing Malt House well.

It was so named because the water was used for the Malt House that was behind the cottages facing the Leicester Road junction. The well may have also been used to supply water to the brewhouse behind the Mansion House (much later to become Jordan's shop). The brewing establishment ceased operation by 1820. The well was looked after and maintained by the Parish Council during the early part of this century until it became redundant in 1924 when mains water was laid along the High Street.

The Primitive Methodist Chapel, opened in 1859.

The chapel was near the bottom of Leicester Road on the left. It was closed in 1963, the congregation having diminished and the building having become unsafe. This photograph was taken after the last service and shows some members of the last congregation.

Swepstone Road, as Leicester Road was still known, in about 1910.

Looking up this quiet road, Mr J W Onions baker and confectioner can be seen walking with his horse and cart. There is no proper footpath on the right-hand side.

Mining subsidence.

Measham has been badly affected by subsidence. The main area subject to damage was north of the church, and little of Leicester Road escaped.

The Ison family
outside their shop in Swepstone Road, 1916.

The off-licence and general store was a few yards from where Mr Onion's cart has been seen previously. Mr Thomas Ison and his wife are shown with their daughters Lizzie and Connie and their son Lewis, who later took over the shop. Lewis was said to measure an ounce of twist tobacco by putting it round his neck like a collar instead of weighing it.

Lewis Ison was the last overseer in Measham for the Poor Law Union. The Union levied a rate annually and normally collected it half yearly, although there were people who refused to pay and were subsequently prosecuted. In his will Mr Lewis Ison left the majority of the ground that he owned in trust, split between the church, the Imperial Cancer Research Fund and the Institute for the Blind. The shop and adjacent row of houses were affected by subsidence and demolished in the mid 1960s.

Measham Colliery.

On the outskirts of the village a mile or so from the bottom of Leicester Road were the Measham mines. Coal has been mined in and around Measham at various periods since at least 1326.

In 1850 two shafts were sunk but later capped over. However a mining engineer named Tate in 1894 formed the Measham Colliery Company, re-opened the shafts and sank them to a depth of 90 yards. The Minorca shaft was not sunk until the 1914-18 war.

The colliery from the spoil heaps.

An early 1960s view of the yard and sidings, which shows that steam locomotives were still in use.

Success crossing the road at Ilott's Wharf in May 1962, with Don Bradbury on the footplate.

Success was built in Scotland by Andrew Barclay of Kilmarnock in 1939, and spent all her life at Measham colliery until she was withdrawn from use and scrapped in May 1964.

The rail connection to the colliery was not made until 1902. Prior to this a horsedrawn tramway to the canal at Ilott's Wharf was used.

Colliers were proud of their steam winding engines and locomotives, and Measham miners were no exception. These engines were lovingly polished and tended as if they were living things. Steam gives a machine life and the driver gets to know his engine and all its habits as a person does with a friend.

Constructing the drift, 1950.

A drift was introduced at the mine in 1950 to provide a direct conveyor outlet from the main underground conveyor to the surface. The drift was a tunnel 400yds long sloping at a gradient of 1 in 4. Another advantage of a drift was that it created a walkable outlet from below ground to the surface, an added safety feature.

The first ranging drum shearer outside the workshops.

In the early 1960s the Measham colliery made significant mining history when the first coal face ranging drum shearer was operated there. The shearer performed well right from the start, having a fair turn of speed. It was christened the "flying flea" by a member of the coal face team.

Standing in front of the shearer are members of the engineering team responsible, they are, left to right, Eddie Turner (enginewright), Ernest Hinks (area mechanisation engineer), and Ivor Pope (assistant enginewright).

The St John's Ambulance Team, winners of the Area Cup in 1935.

The cup had been won against opposition form other local mines, police, firemen and the breweries. The venue for the competition was Ashby Mines Rescue Station and the practice incident had been a mine related accident.

The team members showing off the winners cup are, back row left to right, Mr John Stevens (Colliery Manager), Charlie Ridgeway (shot firer), Robert White (overman), Charles Leigh (under manager), sitting, Eddie Turner (fitter), Harold Buttery (shotfirer), Albert Oakes (shot firer), Jack Wileman (miner).

Measham Colliery underground rescue team, in about 1910.

The team is kitted out in breathing apparatus and with other rescue equipment, ropes, bellows and canary. Some members of the group are known; the man kneeling on the right is Sam Blockley, with Bill Ash kneeling on the left. The man standing second from the right is J. Atkins who was killed in action during the First World War; the colliery manager seated at the front is Mr Wadel.

The last day of operation, 1986.

Sadly the mine was closed in 1986, ending a life of 136 years. With the village having such a long association with mining it is difficult to imagine the way of life without it. No doubt as the scars of the spoil heaps and subsidence disappear it will fade to nothing more than a memory as time passes by.

Measham Hall, from the drive.

Adjacent to the colliery was Measham Hall, with its park, built in 1767 by the Abney family. It remained in their possession until 1924.

The main entrance was at the rear by way of the courtyard. The courtyard was enclosed on one side by the hall on its right, on the left by a series of outbuildings (now cottages). The outbuildings consisted of a laundry and ironing room, a battery room (the hall had a generator and produced its own electricity), a cottage for the chauffeur and others. The top end of the courtyard housed carriages and was later used as garages. A large walled garden was situated to the right of the hall, and used as a kitchen garden and for soft fruit trees.

Sir William de Wiveleslie Abney, K.C.B., D.C.L., F.R.S., Hon. F.R.P.S.

Sir William de Wiveleslie Abney was the last member of the family to reside at the Hall. The family also had a residence at Folkstone where they wintered, having vegetables sent down from Measham during this period of the year. Sir William Abney was best known for his work in the field of photography, particularly the technical chemistry of colour. He was a member of the Royal Photographic Society, becoming its president on no less than three occasions. Sir William was born at Derby in 1843 and died at his Folkstone home in December 1920.

Members of the family and guests posing on the front lawn.

The hall was purchased by the Measham Colliery Company in 1924 and made into separate flats with some of the outside buildings turned into cottages. The main hall was demolished by the National Coal Board in 1959 leaving the converted cottages and lodge still occupied.

Clock Mill in about 1902 with the steam engine in operation.

A little further out of the village stands Clock Mill Farm. It is believed that a mill has stood on this site since the 11th or 12th century. The mill was run from a half acre lagoon fed from the Gilawiskaw stream. The mill had become part of the Abney estate by 1873.

The people are Miss George, the housekeeper, in the doorway with Ethel Haynes. Next to the doorway is Fred Haynes, a miller and a distant cousin. Near the engine shed is Ernest Haynes, then aged eight, and his father, Thomas Haynes, the miller. Mr. Thomas Haynes had been invited by the Abney family to renovate the mill. He did so and remained for 52 years as the miller. The property was later sold (together with much of the Abney estate) to the Measham Colliery Company. Later still, Mr. Haynes, like other tenants, was able to purchase the property.

Clock Mill and farm.

The outline of the lagoon (which provided supplies of water for the water wheel) can be seen towards the top of this aerial photograph.

The mill as a water-mill.

The steam engine was used presumably when the water level in the lagoon was low and there had been a windmill on the site in earlier times for this purpose.

At the rear of the mill, shown here, was the screen and the sluice gate which controlled the flow of water to the mill wheel.

The water-wheel after removal, about 1965

The millhouse as shown in the 1902 photograph was not occupied after 1959 but the mill still continued in use, operated again by water power, until 1964, and then until 1980 it was operated by tractor power.

The millstones were 4 feet in diameter, dressed with grooves in them in such a pattern to work the ground flour out to the edge of the stones. The stones weighed about 1 ton when they were new. A spare set of stones was kept so that one set could be dressed while the other set was being used.

The mill wheel (shown in this photograph, taken during the conversion into living accommodation in 1982/83) was of the overshot type, eleven feet in diameter and six feet wide.

opposite page
Ernest Haynes at work in 1957.

The spare mill wheel can be seen behind Mr. Haynes, although it would appear that the mill by then was only used occasionally. Mr. Haynes still lives at the mill (1990) aged 96.

The Manor House, before demolition, 1969.

On the left hand side of the High Street in the Ashby direction was a large building once known as the Manor House. This house was never a manor but the name was a corruption of Mansion House. It was built in the 1780s or early 90s by Wilkes of his famous 'jumb' bricks. Part of the house was used as the Wilkes bank and the rear premises were a brewing house in the time of William Hill. It later became Jordan's shop and bakehouse.

Outside the Swan in the 1920s.

On the opposite side of the road is the Swan public house, kept
by Harry Rudin from 1913 to 1930. Amongst the group is Harry
Rudin's son on the left, Mr. Jenkins in the centre (with moustache),
Mr. Sindall and Mr. Stanley. The youngster partly hidden is Cyril
Wileman, son of Vince Wileman, the local barber.

The Laurels.

Further along the left hand side of the road was an imposing house known as The Laurels. This large house, standing in a well laid-out garden with wrought iron gates and fencing, is still standing, although sadly not in the same condition now as in this 1903 photograph. One of the owners was the Reverend Mr. Appleton who married the vicar's daughter in 1897. The property is now the Hill Top Cafe.

Children on their way to Willesley for a singing competition.

The group can be seen gathering between The Laurels and the corner of New Street. The house on the extreme right is the one adjacent to the corner. One group from the Baptist chapel under the guidance of Mr. Andy Meaden was awarded first prize for their singing of the hymn 'Sing merrilly sing', composed, appropriately, by Dr. John Buckley, the Measham-born Baptist missionary.

New Road End, 1918.

The junction between New Street and High Street has certainly changed. The house on the left of the corner looks externally very similar today, but the right hand side has seen a number of changes. There was Mr. Pickering's cycle repair workshop which later became his first garage. This building had a curved corrugated sheet roof and a petrol pump outside. Later, the extensive garage that is there today was built.

Recruiting during the First War.

New Street corner was a popular spot for photographs. This one shows a recruiting parade with the men, some in uniform, marching past New Street towards the centre of the village.

opposite page
VE celebrations in 1945.

Between The Laurels and New Street on the opposite side of the road was Saddington's Yard. There was a row of cottages on the right-hand side of the yard, a row of cottages standing back a little facing the road, and a number of outbuildings at the top. Here, Saddington's Yard is being used by the residents of Ashby Road and the top of High Street for their celebrations.

top opposite page
Ashby Road at the turn of the century.

Wood's Yard was next to Saddington's Yard, opposite New Street. Wood's Yard is on the extreme left of this picture.

bottom opposite page
Knitting workers at Ibstock Cottages, 1927.

A short distance from New Street on the right of Ashby Road was a knitting factory which flourished for many years under the ownership of Mr. Walter Grainger. Mr. Grainger started his business at Ibstock Cottages where this photograph of his workforce was taken.

The people are left to right: Mrs. Grainger, Edna Guild (later Mrs. Clifford Hart), Margaret Grainger (the little girl), Doris Bradford (later Mrs. Eric Wheeldon), Kathleen Redfern (later Mrs. Charlie Dennis), Mary Starbuck, Lucy Johnson (later Mrs. Knifton Johnson), Rene Bailey (later Mrs. Freddy Williamson), Pheobe Stanfield (later Mrs. Cyril Peach), Florrie Wileman (later Mrs. Frank Fowkes), and Edna Ridgeway (later Mrs. Jack Trellise).

Mrs. Grainger had come from the Potteries to Measham in 1918 and had brought a stocking knitting machine with her. Later she bought a flat machine to use herself to make jumpers and eventually increased the number of machines and employed a labour force. Mr. Grainger moved his premises from Ibstock Cottages to Ashby Road in 1929.

Five Lane Ends crossroads at the top of Ashby Road in the first decade of the century.

The toll-house was both the home of the toll collector and the collecting place of the tolls charged to travel on the Ashby to Tamworth and the Blackfordby to Ibstock turnpike roads.

Five Lane Ends toll-house.

A slightly earlier photograph, taken from roughly where the pedestrian is sitting in the previous scene. The toll-house was demolished for road widening in the 1950s: its last known resident was a farm worker, Mr. Kirkman.

An Edwardian view of the lower part of the village, looking from the church southwards.

The two groups of people in those traffic-free days are at the corner of Bosworth Road on the left, and outside the Bird in Hand.

High Street in the late 1940s.

The same ornamental lighting post in the left foreground can be seen, but there are a number of modern additions - the telephone box, the road sign and, of course, both moving and parked cars.

Shop assistants of Walker's Stores in the 1920s.

The store, with its neat window displays of tins, stood at the corner of High Street and Queen Street. The assistants are, left to right, Olive Jones, Isabel Hart and Rose Sears.

The Lathams in front of their grocer's shop, 1900.

The shop was a few yards down High Street from the church. The people shown are, left to right, Mr. Joseph Latham, his father Mr. Joseph Latham, the little girl Nora Granger Mason (nee Latham) born 1896, Mrs. Clara Fanny Lathan (née Granger) the wife of the younger Joseph Latham. The young man on the right has not been identified.

CENTRAL STORES,

Measham,   *191*

M

In Account with

LATHAM & SON,

FAMILY GROCERS,

Provision, Corn and Flour Merchants

A bill head from an account book of Latham & Son.

The book is still in the possession of the granddaughter of the younger Mr. Joseph Latham. The shop was then known as the Central Stores and is now the Post Office.

MEASHAM PENNY READINGS.

TEMPERANCE HALL,

On *Thursday, February 14th*, 1867.

PROGRAMME.

1. QUADRILLE ....".Maryland." ....BAND.
2. READING ...." On happiness." ......MR. S. YEOMANS.
3. SONG............................" Land, Land." ....MR. BALL.
4. READING ... { Mrs. Brown at the Royal } MR. J. WHITWORTH.
   { Academy." }
5. PART-SONG... " Hard times come again no more." ....——
6. READING ....MR. T. YEOMANS.
7. SONG ...." The Village Blacksmith." ......MR. J. LEWIN.
8. READING ....REV. W. DYSON.
9. SONG ....MR. GERMAN.
10. READING " A Yung Chap's Coartin Adventures." MR. A. LEWIN.
11. PART-SONG......" Never forget the dear once." ....——
12. READING ....MR. W. C. MOORE.
13. VALSE ...." Claribel." ....BAND.
    " RULE BRITANNIA."

THE CHAIR TO BE TAKEN BY

MR. PEARCE,

AT HALF-PAST SEVEN O'CLOCK.

JNO. BARKER, PRINTER, " STAMP OFFICE," ASHBY.

Penny Readings at the Temperance Hall.

On the opposite side of High Street is the Temperance Hall, built in 1852 at a cost of £100, to which Earl Howe of Gopsall Hall had contributed £10 with a condition that religious teaching should be excluded. The foundation stone was laid by the Rev. J.C. Moore, Archdeacon of the Isle of Man and a former vicar of Measham. Penny Readings, like the one advertised here in 1867, were a popular means in the Victorian period of popular entertainment and education. In latter days, the hall was used exclusively for entertainment, and by 1923 it was a billiard hall. The building has recently been purchased by Age Concern.

Bonas's boot and shoe shop, opposite the Temperance Hall, about 1900.

Notice the boots hanging up at the front of the shop window and by the shop door. Mr. Wright Bonas (with beard), his wife Alice, his daughter Lilian and son Bertram are posing in front of the shop.

Members of the Bonas family have been shopkeepers in Measham since at least 1861, probably in the same premises. Before the buildings became shops they were apparently houses with steps up to them similar to the house on the corner of High Street and Bosworth Road.

The Church Parade in Bosworth Road, 1914.

Bosworth Road has changed less than most of the other streets in the village, except for the right hand corner with High Street, where the properties have made way for a paved area. Local people are watching and following the parade with this section having the Desford Boys' Band, together with members of the local constabulary and fire brigade. The White Hart does not appear to have an inn sign displayed outside as it does today.

The Wesleyan Methodist Chapel of 1840.

The building had an attractive arched entrance to the school rooms. A day school was taught there for a short period of its life but the rooms were later used mainly for a Sunday School until the conversion of the chapel took place. The day school opened in 1871 with 115 pupils on the roll. An extension was built in 1874 but the school closed in 1880.

The chapel school entrance also provided access to the pulpit end of the chapel and to the organ and choir balcony. The congregation balcony had access from the rear of the chapel. This photograph shows the front of the chapel before the schoolrooms were demolished during the alterations which took place (mainly with voluntary labour) during the period 1979 to 1982.

Outside Stanfield's General Draper Stores, 1884.

Next to the chapel was originally a number of cottages dating from about 1790. Later these were converted into shops, owned and run by the Stanfield family. The shops sold drapery, wallpaper, furniture and carpets. The property stayed in the Stanfield family until 1982.

The people are, from the left: Miss Alice Statham who later married Mr. William Stanfield, Miss Mary Ellen Wright (shop assistant), Mr. E. Stanfield and Miss Edith Stanfield (two children in front), Mrs. Katherine Stanfield (Kitty) and the two children with her, George and William Stanfield. The lady on the far right is Lottie Liggins and the gentleman is Luke Liggins.

Brickyard Cottages, formerly the Shed Houses.

Along Bosworth Road, still on the left, standing at approximately 90 degrees to the road, are the Brickyard Cottages formerly known as the Shed Houses or Shed Row. These cottages provide a link with the Wilkes period. They are made of jumb bricks and were originally part of the nearby brickworks of about 1790. The cottages now have garages at ground level with living accommodation above. Originally, the ground floor provided brick-drying sheds used to allow the bricks to dry before firing in the kilns, and the upper floors consisted of a series of inter-connected rooms used as weaving sheds. The conversion to cottages dates from at least 1851.

Bosworth Road in 1910.

The Catholic Church, with its lofty bell tower can be seen. The tower has now been removed. This photograph also shows the solitary gas lamp outside the church, but no sign can be seen of the War Memorial which now stands opposite it. The house next to the church has a stone date tablet of 1874 set into the wall.

A closer view of St. Charles' Church.

The Loudon family from Willesley were considerable patrons of the church and purchased land opposite the church to prevent other buildings being erected and obscuring the view. Later they gave permission for the War Memorial to be sited on that plot of land. The Countess of Loudon attended the church. She is said to have used a coach drawn by a team of cream-coloured horses.

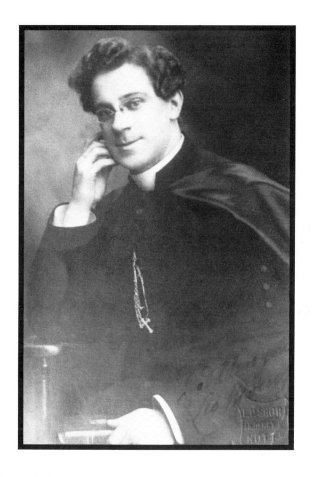

Father Leo Moens as a young man.

Father Moens came to Measham in 1916. He was to play a big part in the religious and general life of the community.

A diamond jubilee and a silver jubilee.

In 1941 St. Charles' Church celebrated its diamond jubilee as well as the 25 years that Father Leo Moens had served as the parish priest. On this occasion a booklet was prepared with this as the front cover.

Father Moens at his gate in later years.

One of Father Moens' favourite pastimes was fishing in the Measham canal. Failing eyesight forced his retirement in 1955.

Measham War Memorial.

Opposite St. Charles is the War Memorial commemorating those who fell in the 1914 - 1918 war. An acre of land was donated by the Earl of Loudon, and the memorial was unveiled by the Countess of Loudon in May 1921. The Portland stone cross was erected as a frontpiece to the shrubbery, tennis courts, bowling green and a children's recreation ground. Many efforts by the local population were devised to raise the £2000 required to pay for the tribute to their fallen friends and relatives. One such effort was to collect enough pennies to stretch for one mile.

The memorial commemorates the 44 men killed in action during the 1914-1918 war and the names of eight men killed in the 1939 - 1945 war were added later. A lime tree was planted for each of the 44 men, with flowering ornamental trees for the other 8. A member of the Home Guard was one of the eight. He was Mr William Williamson, killed by a home-made bomb.

Sir Frank Watson Dyson.

In 1868 Dyson was born in Measham Baptist Manse (now the Catholic church presbytery). He was the eldest son of the Reverend Watson Dyson. The family moved away from Measham in 1870 when Frank was only two years old.

Sir Frank Dyson was educated at Bradford Grammar School and Cambridge. He entered the Royal Observatory at Greenwich as chief assistant in 1894. Five years later he became secretary to the Royal Astronomical Society and in 1901 a Fellow of the Royal Society.

He was made Astronomer Royal for Scotland in 1905 and in 1910 Astronomer Royal for England, knighted in 1915 and retired in 1933. Sir Frank Dyson's main achievements were in the area of stellar motions and in observations of the solar eclipses.

He was largely instrumental in the introduction of the Greenwich time signal. He died in May 1939.

Measham Cemetery Lodge.

At the end of Bosworth Road is the parish cemetery. At the entrance there is a lodge on the right-hand side of the archway and a meeting room on the left. The meeting room has been restored as the parish council room, is used for other small meetings and has been used as a coroner's court room. Note the ornamental railings on top of the front wall. These were taken down as part of the war effort to build armaments as were those of many private dwellings.

The cemetery was opened in 1882 and was controlled by a Burial Board under the chairmanship of Mr Thomas Yeomans. In 1895 the cemetery became the responsibility of the Parish Council. The attractive lodge was built by Mr John Hair of Church Gresley for the sum of £501-16-0 (the lowest tender out of 14) and completed by August 1892. The boundary wall was built by a local builder, Mr George Smith, who also built a number of nearby houses at the top of Bosworth Road.

The first sexton was paid £7-10-0 per year. A tool house was added and a hearse purchased in 1883 at a cost of £19-17-6. It was a hand-pulled type, hired by the mile.

The Junction of High Street and Chapel Street from the end of Bosworth Road in 1907.

The public house sign for the Bird in Hand can be seen to the right of the picture. Next to the Bird in Hand is John Wileman's barber's shop with the general store next door run by the sisters, Misses Alice and Cissie Patrick. On the corner next door is the shop run by Norman Patrick brother to the two sisters. The house on the opposite corner of Chapel Street was pulled down in the 1930s and the building on the extreme left of the photograph (the lower corner of High Street and Bosworth Road) was demolished in the 1960s.

The Baptist Church from Chapel Street about 1906.

On Chapel Street (formerly known as Finches Lane) stands the Baptist Chapel. The first chapel on the site was built in 1811, but later was found to be too small and enlarged in 1823. This first chapel was later replaced in 1841, as it was still too small. The canal had been used formerly for baptisms and when the canal was in existence a step could still be seen where access for baptisms took place. One of the chapel's most notable events was a visit by one of the most well-known religious speakers of his period, the Reverend C.H. Spurgeon, in 1857. Over 1000 gathered for the service, with a special train being laid on from Derby to Moira to carry the extra visitors.

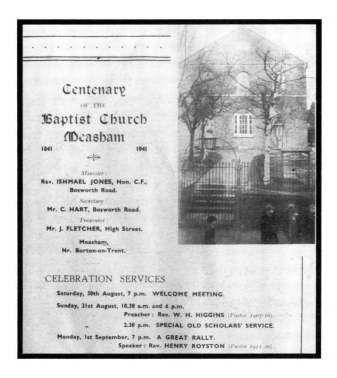

Centenary
OF THE
Baptist Church
Measham
1841   1941
✠

Minister :
Rev. ISHMAEL JONES, Hon. C.F.,
Bosworth Road.
Secretary :
Mr. C. HART, Bosworth Road.
Treasurer :
Mr. J. FLETCHER, High Street.

Measham,
Nr. Burton-on-Trent.

CELEBRATION SERVICES.
Saturday, 30th August, 7 p.m. WELCOME MEETING.
Sunday, 31st August, 10.30 a.m. and 6 p.m.
Preacher : Rev. W. H. HIGGINS *(Pastor 1907-10)*
" 2.30 p.m. SPECIAL OLD SCHOLARS' SERVICE.
Monday, 1st September, 7 p.m. A GREAT RALLY.
Speaker : Rev. HENRY ROYSTON *(Pastor 1911-20).*

The Chapel as it was at the centenary celebrations in 1941.

As well as the then minister, the Reverend Ishmael Jones, two former ministers took part in the celebrations, the Reverend W. H. Higgins (pastor 1907-10) and the Reverend H. Royston (1911-1920).

Dr John Buckley, 1813-1886.

There has been considerable missionary involvement on the part of the Baptist Church, possibly stemming from the fact that a well-known Baptist missionary was born and baptised in Measham.

John Buckley was born in Measham in 1813 and baptised in the canal in 1825. He went to Wisbech College in 1834 and in 1844 sailed to Orissa in India to found the mission there. He married Miss Sarah Derry in India. She was the daughter of the pastor of Barton Fabis. Dr John Buckley died in 1886 and was buried in India where the greater part of his ministerial life had been spent.

He was well known as the translator of the scriptures into Indian languages. He is commemorated at Market Harborough Baptist Church, where he had been pastor before embarking on his missionary work.

Johnson's Stores and Post Office February 1901.

Further down the left-hand side of the High Street was Mr George Johnson's store. His shop at this time incorporated the Post Office. At this period the postal town for Measham was Atherstone and the post was brought daily by horse and trap. We know when the photograph was taken as the newspaper bill on the board outside gives notice of Queen Victoria's funeral.

Mr Johnson also had a printing business at the rear of his shop, access being gained by a driveway leading from Navigation Street. In the window of his shop what looks like sheet music hangs up for sale. Mr Johnson was the church organist and choirmaster. He was also responsible for a number of photographs of old Measham, many which have survived and are reproduced in this collection.

At the doorway of Fletcher's shop.

This was next door to Johnson's, on the corner of High Street and Navigation Street. Standing in the doorway are Mrs Fletcher, Mrs Aston, Ethel Fletcher and Dorothy Sindall.

Thatched cottages on High Street, below Chapel Street.

The thatched cottages, gas lamps and horse drawn vehicles must have added character to the streets, much pleasanter perhaps than the noise and exhaust fumes of today. These cottages were in existence at least until 1907 to judge by another photograph, although this one is of a slightly earlier date.

The Baptist Manse (1874-1894) in Navigation Street.

Navigation Street runs parallel to the line of the old canal and gave access to the rear of the warehouses and malt house, which still survive. These premises were adjacent to the canal and built about 1800. Along the street on the right hand side is a house which was the Baptist Manse from 1874-1892. Standing in front of the house is Miss Annie Fowkes the second daughter of Joe Fowkes, at one time manager of the Coronet Company. This photograph was taken before the Second World War as the railings were then removed for the war effort.

The Wesleyan Reform Chapel.

On the left hand side of Navigation Street was the Wesleyan Reform Chapel. This had a very short life as a place of worship. It was erected in 1870 but no records survive after 1899. The chapel was dedicated by the Reverend W. M. Griffiths of Derby on May 21st 1870.

The chapel building was used as a wholesale grocer's for a while under the ownership of Goodwins and the Registrar used a room there to register births and deaths. Later it was used for many years as a printer's by Mr Lawson Thirlby and latterly by Red Bank for a short period before its eventual demolition in 1981.

Looking down High Street from Navigation Street in Edwardian days.

The men are standing on the corner of Navigation Street. The Loudon Arms is clearly visible, as is evidence of horse-drawn transport.

The buildings on the right were originally built as canal warehouses like the one on the left between the Loudon Arms and the canal bridge. These buildings were erected at the time of Joseph Wilkes as were others in the centre of the High Street. At the time of the photograph the premises would have belonged to, from the left, Thirlby's drapery shop, the Loudon Arms, Mrs Bonas's pot shop and Mr Malcolm's tinsmiths, next to the bridge.

Looking up High Street from the canal bridge in about 1908.

The modern world has begun to impinge on this tranquil scene. No cars are visible, but the comparatively recent telegraph poles are much in evidence.

The canal warehouses on the west side of High Street as they were in 1910.

The ironmonger's shop belonging to the Stanfields later became a draper's shop. The shop was originally a house.

A rear view of the canal warehouse on the west side of High Street.

The canal bridge has been blocked but the smaller warehouse access bridge can still be seen. The Wilkes' curved-top window recesses are again in evidence.

The end of the matching canal warehouse on the east side of the street.

The building on the right at one time was a public house known as The Gate Hangs Well and on its sign it had a rhyme:

This gate hangs well,

and hinders none.

Refresh and pay, and travel on.

The crowd is assembled to watch the fire brigade giving a demonstration. The person on the bridge is about to jump into a blanket.

The Ashby Canal at Measham, looking from High Street to Horse's Lane Bridge.

The Ashby Canal, once such a prominent feature of the village, was authorised by an Act of Parliament in 1794 for a 50 mile long canal from Ashby Wolds to Marston near Coventry. The original estimate was for a construction cost of £23,317 but two years later a new estimate of £100,000 was proposed.

The canal took ten years to be cut and opened in 1804 at a final cost of £166,000 and with a reduced length of 30 miles.

It is interesting to note that in 1815 a company rented warehousing space along the wharf at Measham to build up an export trade in cheese. This was a short lived venture to supply cheese to the Navy. The cheese was made locally at Snarestone.

The canal, looking from the same point in the opposite direction.

The backs of the houses at the bottom of Chapel Street are clearly seen. The ground on the left is where the picture house was constructed in the 1920s. It has latterly become the Youth Club.

High Street bridge from Horse's Lane.

The arches of the main High Street and warehouse bridges can be seen. A favourite pastime of many local people is demonstrated on the tow-path.

An idyllic, though unrepeatable, scene.

This photograph was taken from the towpath under Horse's Lane bridge, again looking towards High Street.

The coaling wharves at the Ilott, having seen better days.

The canal was widened into a basin to allow the barges to turn around for loading. Originally the coal was brought down from the colliery to the wharf by horse drawn tramway and later by rail waggon. Eventually all the coal was transported by rail to the main line.

Wilkes' warehouse alongside the canal.

This warehouse stood near one of Wilkes' other enterprises, boat building. His boatyard was at the bottom of Chapel Street, down the hill past York House. The square building in front of the warehouse was the canal inspector's office, with windows on three sides so he had a good view of the barges and other craft travelling the canal in order to collect the toll charges.

This building has been removed and rebuilt on the Shackerstone preserved railway.

Burton Bridge on the Ashby Canal.

This bridge - officially Meir Bridge - was further on in the Oakthorpe direction.

The Measham stretch of the canal between Donisthorpe and Ilott's Wharf was abandoned in 1957 and filled in with household refuse.

Holland's Palace of Light, ready for customers.

Alongside the canal just by the High Street bridge was built the picture house, a wooden structure of about 1914, probably called The Showbridge.

Before this was built the Holland fairground family used to winter there. To earn money during the winter period Annie Holland, who had married into the fairground family, had a portable Palace of Light built and gave bioscope shows. The Palace of Light was built by Orton and Spooner of Burton in 1911. She took pictures of local people coming out of work and then advertised 'come and see yourself on the big screen'.

In the fens.

The Palace of Light travelled far and wide with its bioscope show. Here it is being towed behind a traction engine, far from home in East Anglia.

The Showbridge becomes the Picture Palace.

Annie Holland eventually had a permanent picture house built and left one of her sons to manage it.

By 1915 The Showbridge had become the Picture Palace as can be seen from this post card advertising a 15 week serial called "The Master Key".

The films came by train from Burton. Some people would wait for the train to arrive before going into the cinema to be certain that their favourite serial would be shown. If the film they were expecting wasn't on the train then they would save their two-pence halfpenny admission.

A gas engine drove the generator to provide light for the projector, which was often operated by Mr Dennis. A mouth organist sometimes provided the music.

In 1932 the cinema was rebuilt in brick and had its name changed yet again, this time to The Empire which remained until its closure. By 1962 The Empire had become a youth club.

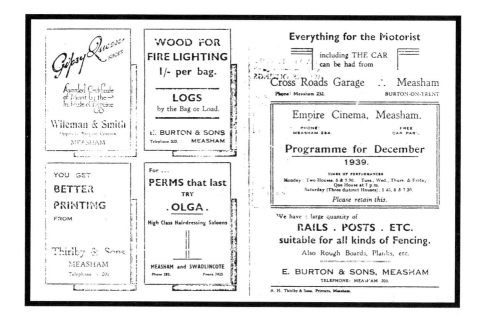

Another change of name.

These advertisements from the Empire Cinema programme for December 1939 contain some still familiar names.

YOUR PALATE WILL TELL YOU THAT

Burbidge's Bread is Best

Specialities :— MILK BREAD (made with Fresh New Milk)
BROWN BREAD, HOVIS.

Discount equal to any.   Van Deliveries Daily.
J. W. BURBIDGE   ::   ::   MEASHAM

Mon. & Tues , Dec. 18 & 19.
Carole Lombard & Frederic March in
NOTHING SACRED
also Comedy Serial & full programme

Wed. & Thurs., Dec. 20 & 21.
Joan Bennett & Henry Fonda in
I MET MY LOVE AGAIN
also Comedy Serial & full programme

Fri. & Sat , Dec. 22 & 23.
Jane Withers & Stuart Erwin in
CHECKERS
also TEXAS SERENADE

Mon., Xmas Day, Dec. 25.
Eddie Cantor in
ALI BABA GOES TO TOWN
also MACUSHLA

Tues., Boxing Day, Dec. 26
Sonja Henie in
ONE IN A MILLION
also SING AND BE HAPPY

Wed., Dec. 27.
Peter Lorre in his best
THANK YOU MR. MOTO
also CHANGE OF HEART

Thursday Programme to be arranged

Fri. & Sat., Dec. 29 & 30.
Dorothy Lamour & Ray Milland in
HER JUNGLE LOVE
also THUNDER TRAIL

JOHN ALEX. MEADEN

CARPENTER, JOINER & UNDERTAKER

Dealer in Boards, Laths and Scantlings.

AGENT FOR HOTPOINT VACUUM CLEANERS. Demonstrations Free.

FUNERALS COMPLETELY FURNISHED.

BOSWORTH ROAD   ::   ::   MEASHAM

A part programme.

Among the films "I was a captive in Germany" will be noticed. This seems to be the only topical item, though. John Alex Meaden, whose advertisement appears, was well-known in the village - as undertakers usually were. Usually known as 'Ander Meaden', he was organist at the Baptist Church for many years. Belfield's, it will be noticed, still provided the service of a more customer-conscious age.

Mr George Hart, saddler, coming out of his shop in the 1950s.

Measham had an association with leather and the tanning of it for many years. The Tanyard situated on the east side of the High Street between the canal and the station drive, was a tanning complex in the Eighteenth Century or possibly earlier. The tanyard cottages (now demolished) were part of the manor bought by Wilkes in 1777. The warehouse (later the Gate Inn) opposite the picture house and the cottages further down (now shops) were built in 1806. The Pinfold (the area behind the supermarket) was the area where the animals were penned while awaiting slaughter. It can be assumed that a butchery was also on the premises. The animals would be skinned and the skin passed to the tannery for processing.

The Tanyard was offered for sale in 1836, but apparently not as a going concern.

Mr Levi Jones, wheelright and some of his wares.

The wheelright's yard was on the west side of High Street, just beyond the Union Hotel.

Levi Jones was born at Gresley in 1855, but came to Measham as a young man. Mr Jones started his business as a wheelright and blacksmith, later adding coachbuilding and undertaking.

During his coachbuilding period he employed an upholsterer and a painter. Levi Jones' son George declined to continue his father's undertaking business so his father set him up in a cycle repair and sales shop in the building opposite (now the supermarket). Mr Levi Jones bought the house between the Tanyard and the Pinfold. This is the house with a portico built in 1778. He converted the property into three houses, presumably one for each child. Mr Jones taught himself to read and write and also owned the first car in Measham, an Overland which was later converted into a lorry.

With the aid of Mr Thomas Hart, Mr Jones organised the Infirmary Parades and made the wooden collecting boxes for these occasions. Mr Levi Jones lived until 1944.

Followers of the Infirmary Parade.

In this view looking from the railway bridge up High Street, Mr Jones' premises can be seen on the left of the road.

George Sears, stationmaster, in his top hat, stands on the platform of Measham's typical Midland Railway station.

The railway through Measham opened in 1873 as the Ashby and Nuneaton Joint Railway, jointly owned by the L.N.W.R. and Midland Railway. The line opened for freight traffic on the first of August 1873 and for passengers on the first of September 1873.

The goods shed, sidings and cattle pen were to the south of the station as was the signal box. Regular passenger trains ceased in April 1931 but freight remained until July 1964. In its final years only coal from the Measham colliery was moved from Measham towards Burton, although some passenger specials had been operated before the war.

Measham Colliery had a connection to the Main line rail sidings installed in 1902, giving a much speedier movement of their coal than by the canal which had been their outlet until then.

Mr Sears started at Measham station when the line opened to passengers in 1873 as a booking clerk. Mr Sears then moved to Overseal, Hugglescote and Ketton before returning to Measham in 1880 as the station master. He retained his position until his retirement in 1922 after 49 years on the railway.

Measham signal box.

The box stood alongside the sidings, south of the station close to Horse's Lane canal bridge. Mr Vaughan is leaning out of the box window with Bill Burton, Walter Pope, Bill Buckley and Teddy Paine on the track. Teddy Paine was the canal inspector. The picture was probably taken in the late 1940s.

The last High Street railway bridge.

The original bridge was a horse-shoe shaped structure which was replaced by this metal bridge in 1922 to allow road widening and give more height for passing traffic. In its turn, the metal bridge was removed in 1985, shortly after this photograph was taken.

Railway View, Measham

Railway View.

Below the railway bridge on the right hand side of the lower High Street is a row of attractive houses known as Railway View. The row was built in 1901, and this photograph of it was taken in 1917.

The 1904 Infirmary Parade.

Railway View can again be seen, together with an impressive number of policemen, firemen, bandsmen, postmen and others.

Edwardian clothes.

These followers of the same parade give us a good idea of the clothes and fashions of the period. It it also possible to see the hedge at the corner of High Street and Burton Road which enclosed the orchard belonging to the Union Inn which stood opposite, out of this picture to the left.

Yew Tree House.

Opposite the lower end of Railway View was a large house known as Yew Tree House. Here lived Mr Wilmot Massey, once the owner of the Red Bank Terracotta Works. This house is now the Working Men's Club

Wilkes' Corn Mill.

Below Mr Massey's residence was the corn mill, a three-storied building erected by Joseph Wilkes as part of his industrial empire. At the rear of the mill was a large engine house which supplied power to the corn mill and also to a carding mill set further back behind the engine house.

The carding mill was burned down in 1836 and the premises were later used as a woodyard. Set in the wall of the corn mill can be seen the commemorative tablet marking the attempt by Sir George Beaumont's private fire brigade to save the two mills. Only the corn mill survived.

When Mr Blake bought the corn mill in 1906 he converted it into living accommodation. The top storey was removed and the original commemorative tablet reinstated in the front wall of the house. The corn mill is still a residence and has been known since Mr Blake's time as The Priory.

The Union Inn, later Ivy House.

On the junction of High Street and Atherstone Road was the large posting inn built by Wilkes in the late 1870s. It was built at the junction of two turnpike roads, and known as The Union Inn. When it ceased to be licensed, it was called Ivy House.

The inn had stabling, a malt house and domestic quarters known as the Cunnery.

The house when it was the residence of Mr Yeomans, had a croquet lawn tennis court and gardens extending up as far as the Cunnery. Fruit trees, soft fruit bushes and a vegetable garden were opposite, on the corner of Burton Road and High Street.

The Cunnery with its central arch.

The arch gave access to the courtyard and stables. The Wilkes 'trademark' of curved-top recessed windows is very obvious. The front part was later converted into cottages, as were the rooms above the stables. The stables themselves found a use as trademen's premises. The building was finally demolished in 1969.

Burton Road and the High Street junction in 1910.

Ivy House lives up to its name in the picture as it can be seen covered with ivy. The white barrier in the grass along the side of the ditch on the right-hand side of the road is where the brook runs under the carriageway.

The Bleach Mill in the 1880s.

The mill was leased in 1774 by Wilkes as a going concern. During the first half of the Nineteenth Century it contained wash wheels, chemical apparatus, starching machines, cisterns and drying houses. It is seen here shortly after it ceased operation in 1883 and before it was converted into cottages. Before the Atherstone Gardens estate was built, the cottages and adjacent bungalow could be reached down a lane which ran down to the river from a point about 300 yards from the High Street end of Atherstone Road.

Waggons at the Red Bank Manufacturing Company in the late 1930s.

Red Bank is towards the end of Atherstone Road. The original company on the site was called the 'Red Bank Brick and Terracotta Works'. This business floundered and was abandoned at about the turn of the century.

During the First World War both Red Bank and the Coronet works were used by the War Department for storage of munitions.

By 1920 the Lysney family took over the neglected works and restarted the business. Seven kilns were in existence at the time the industry restarted, but they were in a poor state and needed rebanding and relining.

By 1925 the company had become a partnership of Lysney and Turner. The Lysney family were still running Red Bank until 1975.

Firing a kiln.

This 1930s photograph shows George Reeves at work.

Loading and setting.

Notice the considerable extent of the works by this period. The worker in the foreground is George Brown.

Inside the ridge-tile sheds.

The workers include Jim Peach, Norris Bladdon, Jess Bladdon and Walter Taylor.

The original Red Bank Terracotta Company was owned by Mr Wilmot Massey who lived at Red Bank House and later at Yew Tree House.

During the Second World War a large part of the Red Bank production consisted of hollow blocks used for building the end walls of the Nissen huts of army and air force barracks. Later their use was extended for the building of camp cinemas and aircraft hangers.

Mr G. A. Hill.

At the junction of Burton Road and Tamworth Road is the site of the vehicle auctions, started and run for many years by Mr G A Hill. Mr Hill started in Measham in 1937 when he bought a garage and derelict petrol station from a bus operator. He built up the business of the garage until the outbreak of war. He then contracted to buy vehicles for the War Department until the end of hostilities. At the end of the war he had a number of vehicles that the War Department did not want, so he auctioned them. He was encouraged by his success to continue the auction sales and was thus able to start the business. Mr Hill finally sold the concern to British Car Auctions in 1961.

The auction site from the air.

The site covered about 50 acres, and both car and commercial vehicle sales were held. Later, caravans, accessories and special item sales were added. The original sale-rooms were of canvas, but later brickwork was added, as can be seen in this photograph of about 1949. Ivy House can be seen in the bottom right-hand corner. The auction ground itself has two large salerooms, and a temporary marquee saleroom, as well as the filling station and garage, the offices and a large parking area. On the left of the auction site can be seen the shoe factory, gas works, the White House. Westlake Cottages, and Avenue House (by this time a transport cafe). These notable buildings have now all gone, as the auction site has expanded and the industrial estate has been developed.

The wooden structure of the original gatehouse in Burton Road.

The No 1 saleroom, which still incorporates some canvas, is in the background. The Rover car belonged to Mr Frank Elliott. He was starting his journey with three colleagues to open a car auction at Zuttphen in Holland in 1949.

The view from Ivy House.

The auction business is still using marquees and tents, and an impressive number of 1950s vehicles is on show.

Ivy House from the car auction site, 1950.

These cars, in the No 1 Saleroom marshalling area, seem to be grouped by make and model. As well as Ivy House, the gatehouse on Burton Road may be seen.

Considering an important purchase.

This slightly later photograph also shows caravans parked on the car-park at the junction of Burton Road and Tamworth Road. Ivy House can again be clearly seen.

The opening of the Midland Motor Museum.

In 1963 the car auctions were held in high enough esteem by the motor trade to attract the opening of a motor museum.

The exhibits comprised individually owned vehicles and others from the collection of Lord Montagu, with vehicles being rotated with those from his collection at Beaulieu.

Programme of Events

11.30 a.m.   Cars arrive.

12.00 p.m.   Formal Opening inside the Museum by Sir William Lyons, Chairman and Managing Director of Jaguar Cars Ltd.

1.00 p.m.   The general public will be admitted to the Museum.

2.00 p.m.   Parade of Historic Cars led by Sir William Lyons in a 1911 Daimler.

3.30 p.m.   Prize Giving by Sir William Lyons.

Open Throughout the Year

SUMMER (April-October) 10.30 a.m.-6.00 p.m.

WINTER (November-March) 10.00 a.m.-5.00 p.m.

Admission: Adult 3/-   Child 1 6

Special reduced rates for parties.

All enquiries to the Secretary.

Midland Motor Museum, Measham, Burton-on-Trent

Telephone: Measham 575

Open throughout the year, but sadly not for many years.

The Midland Motor Museum lasted only a short while in spite of the opening ceremony having been performed by Sir William Lyons, the Chairman of Jaguar Cars Ltd. A parade of 50 cars took place after the opening, ranging from a 1899 Benz to a 1939 Jaguar. The parade was led by Sir William driving a 1911 Daimler.

The Avenue,
Measham.

top opposite page
The White House, Tamworth Road.

Behind the White House was the original shoe factory. A new factory was built later between the White House and the entrance to the gas works. Tamworth Road was often known as 'The Avenue' at the turn of the century.

bottom opposite page
The front entrance to White House.

White House was built at the same time as the Wilkes mills in about 1783, and was lived in by successive mill owners for many years.

One of the occupiers of White House was Thomas Jewsbury, for a time a partner of Joseph Wilkes.

Two of the Jewsbury daughters became well known writers, Geraldine was a novelist and Maria Jane a poet. A book of poems, novels and essay sketches, some with relevance to Measham, was published in 1825 and called Phantasmagoria. The girls, who were born at White House, moved to Manchester in 1818 when Geraldine was only six.

The house in these years had square brick chimneys, a brick screening wall with an ironwork fence, holly bushes and vines growing up the wall. White House was eventually converted into flats but was demolished in 1977.

Guests at Mr R. B. Hammersley's garden party, 26 July 1919.

The party for his employees at the shoe factory was to commemorate the peace.

After tea entertainment was given and sports activities took place "enjoyed by all concerned". In the evening dancing was arranged and finally the band played."For he's a jolly good fellow", in which all the guests joined.

Mr Hammersley had started the shoe factory in 1902 and ran it until he sold it in 1923. During the Second World War production was switched to military gaiters. Shoe production was resumed after the war until the factory's eventual closure in the late 1960s.

Avenue House while in use as a café.

Avenue House stood slightly back from the road below White House. It was used by various mill managers or owners of other enterprises at the Tamworth Road site. One resident was Mr Hammersley. The gardens were large and at one period joined those of White House. Avenue House was contemporary with White House, although its final use was as a café, mainly a transport café. It was demolished in the early 1960s.

The Avenue, Measham (Tamworth Road), about 1910.

Avenue House can be seen on the left behind the trees and fence, with the White House gable end showing through the trees a short distance further on. The spinney on the right has now given place to Riverway.

Sports Day in the 1930s.

A sports day was held every year from 1918 until the 1930s. The event was held on the ground beyond Avenue House, where the Westminster Industrial Estate now stands. It started off as a local community activity with items such as egg and spoon races etc.

Later the event grew in importance and was held under the regulations of the Amateur Athletic Association and other organisations. Eventually the sports continued under the organisation of the British Legion. Track, field and cycling events were held and competitors came from far afield.

Remains of the main Wilkes mill, 1901.

Behind White House stood the complex built by Joseph Wilkes. The main mill was a large structure built in 1783, with some of it being of three stories. At first the mill machinery was driven by water, but later an atmospheric engine and finally a Boulton and Watt steam engine were installed.

Surveying the damage.

The main mill was eventually used as a tape manufactury, but was burnt down in 1904. Even the damaged remains, however, give an idea of the size and complexity of Wilkes original conception.

The Avenue looking towards the village.

From the bridge over the Mease, the factory chimney and some of the other buildings can be clearly seen, The photograph was presumably taken a few years before the fire.

Measham from Birds Hill, from a painting by L. Villiac, 1806.

Villiac was a prisoner of war who was interned with other Napoleonic War prisoners at Old Parks, Ashby.

The Tamworth Road complex built by Joseph Wilkes in 1783 can be clearly seen on the left of the Avenue. On the right is the new mill built in 1802 on the right of lower High Street. Ivy House can just be seen and the Cunnery is shown to the right of the new mill. The church standing on the brow of the hill is as conspicuous as it is today. On the extreme lower right of the picture is a building which is probably the row of cottage half way up Bird's Hill, once used to house the children working at the mills, and so sometimes called the workhouse. The road across the front of the view is possibly the drive to Side Hollows Farm.

Measham is best known today as the home of one of the biggest car auctions in the country, but it has had an exciting history as a small market town, as a long-standing mining area and as the site of early cotton mills and canalside industries.

This collection of phtographs shows Measham and its people at work and play during the last hundred years. There are shots of the railway, the canal, the colliery and the mill and it shows sportsmen, workers, school children and soldiers as well as many other local characters and activities.

J. S